M000032385

Graduation

Illustrations by
Rebecca Gibbon

RUNNING PRESS
PHILADELPHIA · LONDON

A Running Press Miniature Edition™
© 2000 by Running Press
Illustrations © by Rebecca Gibbon
All rights reserved under the Pan-American
and International Copyright Conventions

Printed in China

Library of Congress Cataloging-in-Publication Number 99-74352

ISBN 0-7624-0705-0

This book may be ordered by mail from the publisher.
Please include $1.00 for postage and handling.
But try your bookstore first!

Running Press Book Publishers
125 South Twenty-second Street
Philadelphia, Pennsylvania 19103-4399

Visit us on the web!
www.runningpress.com

Contents

Introduction

It is possible
to believe that all
the past is but
the beginning of
a beginning. . . .

H. G. Wells (1866–1946)
English writer

CHAPTER

2

Congratulations graduate! This is a very special day, a special time. It's a time to reflect on all the challenges you've faced and all the goals you've accomplished. Remember your first few weeks at school? You were probably very excited and a little nervous, thinking of the mountain that lay ahead of you. And now here

you are at the top of that mountain;
your future is a magnificent vista
with endless opportunities. Enjoy
this moment!

Maybe you already know
what you want to do with your life,
or maybe you're still considering
all the possibilities. . . . Either way,
you now possess the confidence to
set goals, work hard, and ultimately
to trust your own judgment.

Inside this book are quotes
from a wide variety of people—
writers, educators, politicians,
musicians, artists, business people, actors, and more—that will
inspire you, challenge you, and
offer wisdom that is especially
compelling at this crossroads
in your life. Many of these quotes
are taken from memorable
commencement speeches; others

come from the world at large.
They speak of humanity, individuality, and your future . . . and
the last chapter adds a touch of
humor to put it all in perspective.

As you read these pages,
take time to reflect on where you
have been and where you are
going. It's all coming together at
this moment. Make the most of it!

Humanity

The only thing
worth living for is
the lifting up
of our fellow men.

Booker T. Washington (1856–1915)
American educator

From a commencement speech
at Tuskegee Institute, 1891

As you take leave of
[your school], as you graduate
into a new life of the mind, may
each of you ask yourself this:
What am I doing to increase
the sum hope of the world? . . .
What am I doing to teach some-
one else what I have learned?

Arthur Burns (1904–1987)
Austrian-American economist

From a commencement speech
at Hebrew University (Jerusalem), 1970

Each of us can make
the path smoother
for people who follow—
enabling them to
push the envelope
of success and achieve-
ment even further.

Hazel O'Leary
American politician

h u m a n i t y

In the final analysis, our most
basic common link is that
we all inhabit this small planet.
We all breathe the same air.
We all cherish our children's future.
And we are all mortal. . . .

John F. Kennedy (1917–1963)
American president

From a commencement speech
at American University, 1963

For me, words
are a form
of action,
capable of
influencing
change.

Ingrid Bengis
American writer

Each time a man stands up for an
ideal, or acts to improve the lot
of others, or strikes out against
injustice, he sends forth a tiny
ripple of hope, and crossing each
other from a million different cen-
ters of energy and daring, those
ripples build a current that can
sweep down the mightiest walls
of oppression and resistance.

Robert F. Kennedy (1925–1968)
American politician

I think T. S. Eliot was absolutely
right when he wrote in 1919
that tradition is not something
you inherit. If you want it,
you must obtain it with great labor.

Cornel West
American educator

From a commencement speech
at Haverford College, 1994

There are incalculable resources in the human spirit, once it has been set free.

Hubert H. Humphrey (1911–1978)
American vice president

Life lived in freedom is personal responsibility. . . .

Martin Buber (1878–1965)
German-Jewish philosopher

The price of
freedom is
responsibility, but
it's a bargain,
because freedom
is priceless.

Hugh Downs
American journalist

If America is to remain a first-class nation, she can no longer have second-class citizens.

Dr. Martin Luther King, Jr. (1929–1968)
Civil rights leader

From a commencement speech
at Lincoln University, 1961

Today it is true that all can ride
at the front of the bus,
but that's not enough. We must
have a fair chance to drive
that bus . . . to own that bus . . .
and to own that bus company.

Walter Mondale
American vice president

From a commencement speech
at Clark College, 1983

Humans have got
to have confidence.
You have got to
help give it to them.

Dwight D. Eisenhower (1890–1969)
American president

From a commencement speech
at Dartmouth College, 1953

*Even the most
ordinary life is a
mystery if you
look close enough.*

Kennedy Fraser
American essayist

How many of us know a poor
family well enough to go to their
house and have a cup of coffee
and get to know the names of
their teenaged kids? Or—God
forbid—invite them to our house
and maybe take them to a
baseball game or a movie with
our children? Very few.

Jimmy Carter
American president

From a commencement speech
at Duke University, 1997

We have for a full life-time taught our children to be go-getters. Can we now say to them that if they want to be happy they must be go-givers?

Mario Cuomo
New York governor

From a commencement speech
at Iona College, 1984

There are always a lot of people
so afraid of rocking the
boat that they stop rowing.
We can never get ahead that way.

Harry S. Truman (1884–1972)
American president

From a commencement speech
at Howard University, 1952

As life is action and
passion, it is required
that we should share the
passion of our time
at the peril of being
judged not to have lived.

Oliver Wendell Holmes (1841–1935)
American jurist

In youth we learn;
in age
we understand.

Marie Von Ebner-Eschenbach (1830–1916)
Austrian writer

The expansion of
knowledge makes for an
expansion of faith,
and the widening of the
horizons of the mind
the widening of belief.

Norman Cousins (1915–1990)
American editor

A book must be the ax for the frozen sea inside us.

Franz Kafka (1883–1924)
Czech-born German writer

Here [at Kean State College]
you have discovered that so
long as books are kept open,
then minds can never be closed.

Katherine D. Ortega
American (former) representative
to the United Nations

From a commencement speech
at Kean State College, 1985

Individuality

There's only one
corner of the universe
you can be certain
of improving, and
that's your own self.

Aldous Huxley (1894–1963)
English writer

It's when
we're given choice
that we sit
with the gods and
design ourselves.

Dorothy Gilman
American writer

individuality

Your character is what
you are to yourself,
not what you pretend to
be to yourself or others.

John McCain
American senator

From a commencement speech
at Ohio Wesleyan University, 1997

I've never contradicted anybody. My object in life has been to hold my own with whatever's going—not against, but with—to hold my own.

Robert Frost (1874–1963)
American poet

As individuals each
of us must choose
whether to live our lives
narrowly, selfishly, and
complacently, or to act
with courage and faith.

Madeleine Albright
American secretary of state

From a commencement speech
at Mount Holyoke College, 1997

Ambitious   Selfish

complacent

Be different—if you don't
have the facts and
knowledge required,
simply listen.

Ed Koch
American (former) mayor
of New York City

From a commencement speech
at Roger Williams University, 1996

Ask questions.

Susan Sarandon
American actress

From a commencement speech
at Rutgers University, 1993

Go around asking a lot of damn-fool questions. Only through curiosity can we discover opportunities.

Clarence Birdseye (1886–1956)
American inventor

I have a sense of
these buried lives
striving to come
out through me to
express themselves.

Margie Piercy
American poet

If you want something
to change, you
personally have to do
something different.
Defy your own group.
Rebel against yourself.

Cathy Guisewite
American cartoonist

From a commencement speech at the
University of Michigan, 1994

As human beings,
our greatness
lies not so much
in being able to
remake the world . . .
as in being able
to remake ourselves.

Mahatma Gandhi (1869–1948)
Indian leader

What I look for is not
how to gain a firm hold
on myself and on life,
but primarily how
to live a life that would
deserve and evoke
an eternal "Amen."

Abraham Heschel (1907–1972)
Jewish-American philosopher

individuality

In playing ball, or life, a person occasionally gets the opportunity to do something great. When that time comes, only two things matter: being prepared to seize the moment and having the courage to take your best swing.

Hank Aaron
Major League Baseball legend

From a commencement speech at
Emory University School of Law, 1995

It takes great courage to faithfully follow what we know to be true.

Sara E. Anderson
American writer

. . . dream a little before you think and solve.

Toni Morrison
American writer

From a commencement speech
at Sarah Lawrence College, 1988

The only
real elegance is
in the mind.
If you've got that,
the rest
follows from it.

Diana Vreeland
American editor

It is not the mountain we conquer, but ourselves.

Sir Edmund Hillary
New Zealand mountaineer

We do not change as
we grow up. The difference
between the child and
the adult is that the former
doesn't know who
he is and the latter does.

W. H. Auden (1907–1973)
American poet

You need to claim the events of
your life to make yourself yours.
When you truly possess
all you have been and done,
which may take some time,
you are fierce with reality.

Florida Scott-Maxwell (1883–1978)
English psychologist

One cannot divine nor forecast
the conditions that will make
happiness; one only stumbles
upon them by chance, in a
lucky hour, at the world's end
somewhere, and holds fast to
the days, as to fortune or fame.

Willa Cather (1873–1947)
American writer

If you value the world simply for
what you can get out of it,
be assured that the world will in
turn estimate your value
by what it can get out of you. . . .
If you pursue truth,
people will be true to you.

**Arthur Twining Hadley (1856–1930)
Yale University president**

**From a commencement speech
at Yale University, 1903**

Just live in the mess.
Throw yourself out into the
convulsions of the world.
I'm just telling you to live in it,
to look at it, to witness it.
Try and get it. Take chances.
Make your own work, take pride
in it. Seize the moment.

Joan Didion
American writer

From a commencement speech
at Bard College, 1987

[The world] demands the qualities of youth: not a time of life but a state of mind, a temper of the will, a quality of the imagination, a predominance of courage over timidity, of the appetite for adventure over the love of ease.

Robert F. Kennedy (1925–1968)
American politician

Toward the Future

We must be willing to get
rid of the life we've
planned, so as to have the
life that is waiting for us.

Joseph Campbell (1904–1987)
American mythologist

You have played—now comes
work . . . and with the
lifework chosen, remember that
it can become, as you will it,
drudgery or heroism, prosaic
or romantic, brutal or divine.

W. E. B. DuBois (1868–1963)
American historian and educator

From a commencement speech
at Fisk University, 1898

You hold all our futures in your hands. So you better make it good.

Jodie Foster
American actor

From a commencement speech
at Yale University, 1993

I expect to spend the rest
of my life in the future,
so I want to be
reasonably sure what
kind of future it is
going to be. That is my
reason for planning.

Charles Kettering (1876–1958)
American industrialist

If you don't like the
way the world is,
you change it.
You have an obliga-
tion to change it.
You just do it
one step at a time.

Marian Wright Edelman
American writer

To live is to change; to be perfect is to have changed often.

John Henry Newman (1801–1890)
English cleric

Change is the law of life. Those who look only to the past or present are certain to miss the future.

John F. Kennedy (1917–1963)
American president

I don't know whether
this is the best of times
or the worst of times,
but I assure you it's the
only time you've got.

Art Buchwald
American humorist

From a commencement speech
at the University of San Diego, 1976

The aim of life is to live, and to live means to be aware, joyously, drunkenly, serenely, divinely aware.

Henry Miller (1891–1980)
American writer

The future doesn't
belong to
the fainthearted;
it belongs
to the brave.

Ronald Reagan
American president

What's courage
but having
faith instead
of fear?

Michael J. Fox
Canadian actor

Those who cannot remember the past are condemned to repeat it.

George Santayana (1863–1952)
American philosopher

Perhaps we fear having
a past and burn it behind
us like rocket fuel,
always looking forward.

Ken Burns
American filmmaker

From a commencement speech
at Hampshire College, 1987

Men may rise on
stepping-stones
Of their dead selves
to higher things.

Alfred, Lord Tennyson (1809–1892)
English poet

The secret
of success
is constancy
to purpose.

Benjamin Disraeli (1804–1881)
British prime minister

In the dark times when, you know, stuff ain't going right, if you have something to hold on to, which is yourself, you'll survive it.

Whoopi Goldberg
American actor and comedian

From a commencement speech at the University of Vermont, 1997

Of all the forces that make for
a better world, none is so
indispensable, none so powerful
as hope. Without hope men
are only half alive. With hope
they dream and think and work.

Charles Sawyer
American educator

You are not helpless and you're not heartless, and you have time.

Toni Morrison
American writer

From a commencement speech
at Sarah Lawrence College, 1988

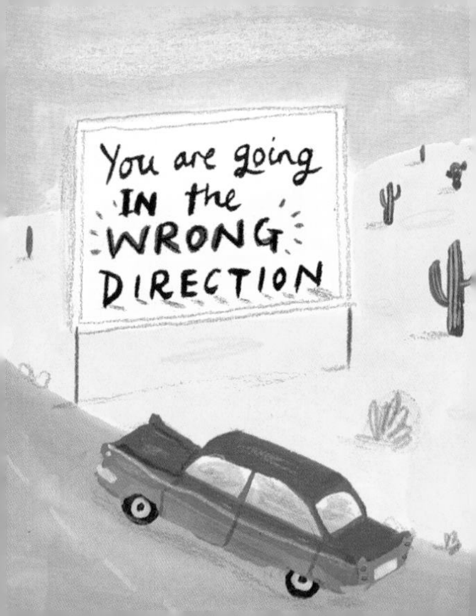
You are going
IN the
WRONG
DIRECTION

You'll make mistakes.
Some [people] will call them
failures, but I have
learned that failure is
really God's way of saying,
"Excuse me, you're
moving in the wrong direction."

Oprah Winfrey
American television host and actor

From a commencement speech
at Wellesley College, 1997

Direct your eye right
inward, and you'll
find a thousand regions
in your mind yet
undiscovered. Travel
them and be expert
in home-cosmography.

Henry David Thoreau (1817–1862)
American writer

Failures are either
those who
do not know what
they want or
are not prepared
to pay the price
asked them.

W. H. Auden (1907–1973)
American poet

We find what we
search for—or,
if we don't find it,
we become it.

Jessamyn West (1907–1934)
American writer

As for me, I know of nothing else but miracles.

Walt Whitman (1819–1892)
American poet

A Sense of Humor

I tell you, with the job market you're facing, you're a terrific audience.

Jerry Seinfeld
American comedian

From a commencement speech
at Queens College, 1994

All of us should feel very proud of ourselves—and just a little bit silly.

Kermit the Frog
American Muppet

From a commencement speech at
Long Island University, upon receiving a
"Doctorate of Amphibious Letters," 1996

You're college graduates
now, so use your
education. Remember:
It's not who you know,
it's whom.

Joan Rivers
American comedian

From a commencement speech
at the University of Pennsylvania, 1989

Do not listen to those who say,
"You're taking too big a chance."
If he did not take a big chance,
Michelangelo would have painted
the Sistine floor and it would
surely be rubbed out today.

Neil Simon
American playwright

From a commencement speech
at Williams College, 1984

Women are told today that they
can have it all, career, marriage,
and children, and I'd like to tell
you that if the word "all" meant
career, marriage, and children,
then you can have it. . . .

Beverly Sills
American opera singer

From a commencement speech
at Smith College, 1985

People will frighten you about a
graduation . . . because they use
words you don't hear often . . .
"And be with you Godspeed."
It is a warning, "Godspeed."
It means you are no longer
welcome here at these prices.

Bill Cosby
American comedian

From a commencement speech
at Southern Methodist University, 1995

Life is rough for everyone. . . .
Life isn't always fair.
Whatever it is that hits the fan,
it's never evenly distributed—
some always tend to
get more of it than others.

Ann Landers
American columnist

From a commencement speech
at Southwestern Adventist College, 1987

If you ever think you're too small to be effective, you've never been in bed with a mosquito.

Anita Roddick
English entrepreneur

From a commencement speech
at Trinity College of Vermont, 1996

If you turn up forty,
drunk and maudlin at
parties talking about how
great everything was
when you were in school,
man, you are one sick puppy.

Stephen King
American writer

From a commencement speech
at the University of Maine, 1987

The best advice I can
give anybody
about going into the
world is this: Don't do it.
I have been out
there and it is a mess.

Russell Baker
American writer

From a commencement speech
at Connecticut College, 1995

graduation

Avoid fatty foods. Avoid smoking,
drugs, Bensonhurst,
the Gaza Strip, bungee jumping,
humorless people,
bad music, fashion, weight
training, and hair-care products.

Chevy Chase
American actor

From a commencement speech
at Bard College, 1990

We wanted to bring you
up with information about sex
that we never had.
Our parents only told us that
if we listened to rock 'n' roll,
we would have babies,
and they were right. You are them.

Garrison Keillor
American writer and broadcaster

From a commencement speech
at Gettysburg College, 1987

g r a d u a t i o n

I graduated with a class committed
to open love, open thinking,
open everything. . . . Twenty-two
years later, the people of my class
are getting cash out of a machine,
dinner out of a clown's mouth,
and it isn't even possible to
get a human being on the phone
at the phone company.

Cathy Guisewite
American cartoonist

From a commencement speech at the
University of Michigan, 1994

graduation

Get out there, work hard,
and thank God we're
living in a country where
the sky's the limit,
the stores are open late,
and you can shop in bed
thanks to television.

Joan Rivers
American comedian

From a commencement speech at the
University of Pennsylvania, 1989

*Recalling advice from the president of
St. John's University (his alma mater):*

"Commencement speakers,"
said Father Flynn, "should think
of themselves as the body
at an old-fashioned Irish wake.
They need you in order to
have the party, but nobody
expects you to say very much."

Mario Cuomo
American (former) governor of New York

From a commencement speech
at Iona College, 1984

*I've played nuns
and hookers,
but I've never worn
a gown like this.*

Lynn Redgrave
English actor

From a commencement speech
at Baruch College, 1995

124

Last night, I dreamt . . . I was greeted with a chorus of boos. A young lady came up with a note on which was written, "How dare you accept this invitation to make the commencement address when you are merely holding on to the coattails of the accomplishments of your wife."

Paul Newman
American actor

From a commencement speech
at Sarah Lawrence College, 1990

Remember
that whatever you
do in life,
ninety percent is
half mental.

Yogi Berra
American baseball legend

From a commencement speech
at Montclair State University, 1996

This book has been bound using
handcraft methods and
Smyth-sewn to ensure durability.

The dust jacket and interior were
illustrated by Rebecca Gibbon.

The dust jacket and interior were
designed by Corinda Cook.

The text was edited by Greg Jones.

The text was set in Monotype Script
and Stempel Schneidler.